Letter to Parents

Dear Parents,

For the past 20 years, I have worked in divorce mediation and served as a Marriage and Family Therapist. In that time, I've helped countless clients navigate the difficult waters of divorce—and learned that, as tough as it is for adults to go through the pain and stress of this process, it is often even harder for their children.

Unfortunately, divorce is an all-too familiar topic for many adults. But for children, it is a foreign concept—one that brings with it a host of fears, insecurities and questions. Over the years, I've had the opportunity to observe and learn from so many children of divorce. Now, I'm delighted to introduce the Fables of Fairy Good Heart™ book series in an effort to help those children and their families, encourage open communication, and keep the parent/child relationship strong.

How to Use this Book
Each book in the Fables of Fairy Good Heart™ series comes with a unique feature to facilitate easy dialogue between parents and their children. You'll find these sections, called "Parent Prompts," at the end of each book chapter.

Each "Parent Prompt" section begins with a summary of the completed chapter, and includes simple questions related to the book's primary child character that are designed to help parents initiate important discussions with their children. By reading the story chapters and "Parent Prompt" sections together, parents and children can broach challenging topics, learn new coping skills, and create a stable environment to reassure children about their place and value in the world.

Whether you and your spouse are getting a divorce, initiating a trial separation, or simply seeking a way to introduce your children to the concept of divorce, the Fables of Fairy Good Heart™ are designed to put children at ease asking questions and sharing their feelings—and to remind them that, no matter what, their parents will love them, "forever and ever, and ever and ever!"

Warmly,

Nancy Fagan
Founder, Fairy Good Heart LLC

Copyright © 2015
All rights reserved. No part of this book shall be reproduced, stored in a retrieval system, or transmitted by any means, electronic, mechanical, photocopying, recording, or otherwise, without written permission from the publisher. No patent liability is assumed with respect to the use of the information contained herein. Although every precaution has been taken in the preparation of this book, the publisher and author assume no responsibility for errors or omissions. Neither is any liability assumed for damages resulting from the use of information contained herein. For information, address FGH Publishing, Info@FGHpublishing.com.

International Standard Book Number (ISBN): 978-0-9908606-2-4

Library of Congress Control Number: 2014919686
Printed in the United States of America

Note: This publication contains the opinions and ideas of its author. It is intended to provide helpful and informative material on the subject matter covered. It is sold with the understanding that the author and publisher are not engaged in rendering professional services in the book. If the reader requires personal assistance or advice, a competent professional should be consulted.

The author and publisher specifically disclaim any responsibility for any liability, loss or risk, personal or otherwise, which is incurred as a consequence, directly or indirectly, or the use and application of any of the contents of this book.

Author: Nancy Fagan
Illustrator: Tory Marshall
Publisher: FGH Publishing
Editor: Lauren Westerfield
Jr. Editors: Kristin Wu and Jessica Pham

FGH Publishing
www.FGHpublishing.com

Parent Kiss Notes

Divorced parents commonly worry that their children will miss them when they are at the other parent's home. Parent Kiss Notes are a way for kids to feel connected, no matter where they are.

How to Use
Tear off a note for each child, write a special note on the back, and then seal it with a kiss. Tuck it in your child's suitcase and tell your child to read it each time homesickness sets in. If you have a Fairy Good Heart™ stuffed toy, you can tuck the note into the "Parent Pocket" along with your photo so you can be with your child at all times. This will bring your child comfort and give you peace of mind.

Sealed with a Kiss

Sealed with a Kiss

Sealed with a Kiss

Sealed with a Kiss

Sealed with a Kiss

Sealed with a Kiss

Dear _____,	Dear _____,
Love _____	Love _____
Dear _____,	Dear _____,
Love _____	Love _____
Dear _____,	Dear _____,
Love _____	Love _____

Fables of
FAIRY GOOD HEART™
Divorce-A Parent's Love Lasts Forever

by Nancy Fagan, Founder of Fairy Good Heart LLC

Illustrated by Tory Marshall

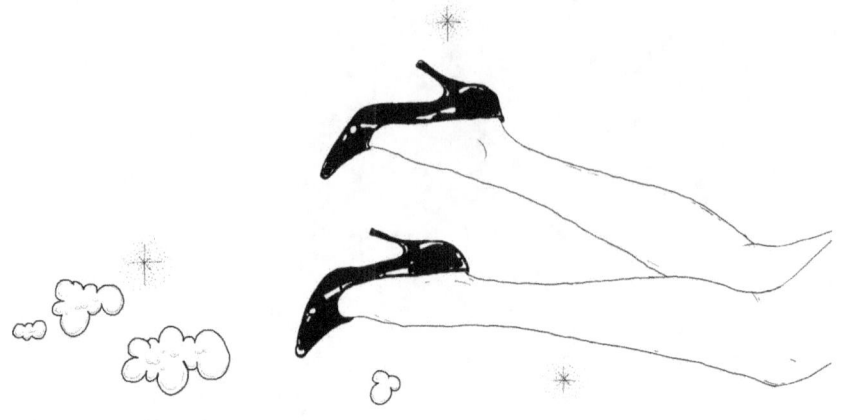

Fable

[fey-buh l] A short tale to teach a moral lesson.

Table of Contents

Chapter 1: The Longest Night
Chapter 2: The Bad News
Chapter 3: Moving Day
Chapter 4: Two Houses for Jaci
Appendix: Fun Stuff for Kids

CHAPTER ONE

The Longest Night

This is a story about a girl named Jaci, and her Mom and Dad who loved her very, very much. Growing up, Jaci didn't have brothers or sisters. It was just Jaci, her Mom and her Dad—and together, the three of them went on lots of adventures, to the zoo or camping or long bike rides along the beach.

Jaci loved her parents, and they made her feel extra special. But she also had lots of friends at school, including her three best friends—Jessica, Amanda-Mia and Brandon, the cutest boy in her class.

Jaci's friends were all very different: Brandon was quiet, and liked to draw pictures of his dog, while Jessica was always laughing and a great swimmer.

Amanda-Mia had two houses, one with her Mom and one with her Dad. And while Jaci always wondered about those two houses, she'd never asked Amanda-Mia about it before.

After all,
Amanda-Mia could do cartwheels
and had a pet hamster.
She was happy,
just like all of Jaci's friends.

Jaci was happy, too. Every day at school was a new adventure, and every night her parents would tuck her into bed and she would fall asleep with a big smile on her face.

But then, one night, things changed.

Something was different. As she lay in bed, Jaci heard loud voices from downstairs.

It sounded like her parents were fighting.

In the dark of her room, the sound of her parents yelling echoed loudly against her walls. Jaci was frightened. She covered her ears and buried her head under the covers.

"Maybe it's just a bad dream," she thought to herself. But the next night the fighting continued, and then the night after that, and the next night again.

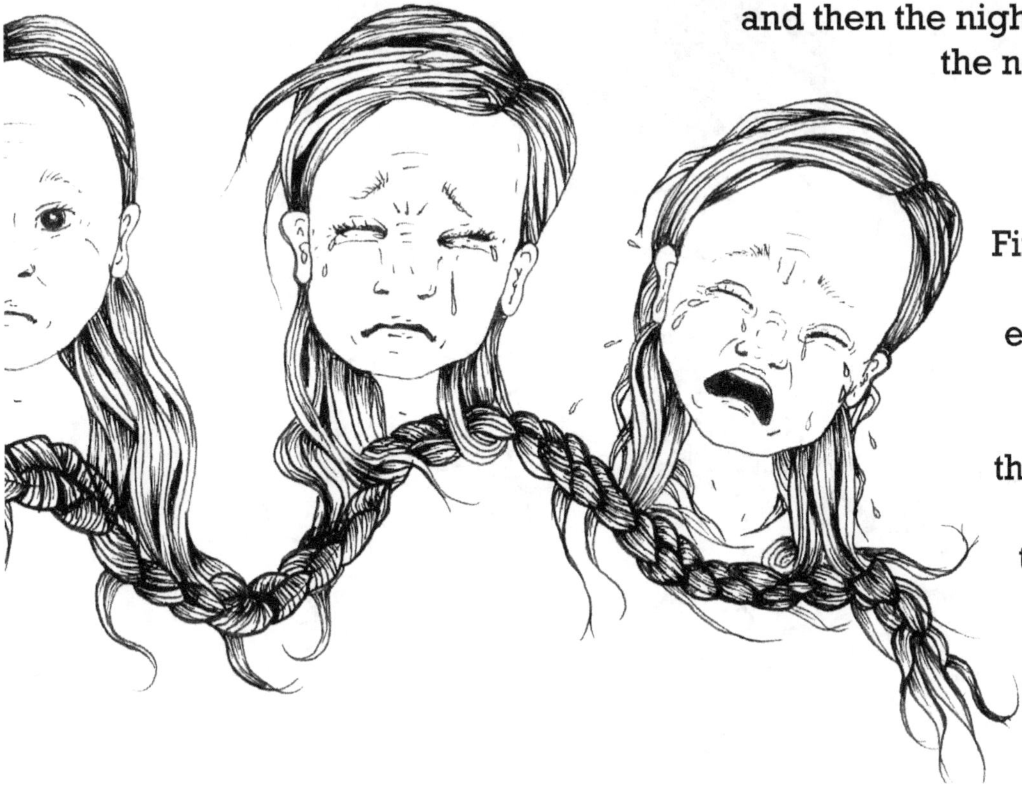

Finally, after what seemed like an endless string of long nights, there came the longest night: the night when the voices grew louder and louder

until at last she heard the words...

"I don't love you anymore!" And then something else —something she didn't understand:

"I want a divorce!"

Jaci didn't know what a divorce was, but she knew it must be horrible. She plugged her ears and closed her eyes the tightest she'd ever squeezed them. She wished she could pretend away the things she'd heard. She felt very sad and afraid—but more than anything else, she felt …

alone.

"If my parents can stop loving each other, can they stop loving me, too?" Jaci wondered.

She started to cry, one tear sneaking down her cheek, then another and another.

Just as she reached up to wipe away her tears, something **magical** began to happen. Where a moment ago there had been nothing but darkness and fear, there was now a bright light the color of cotton candy and glitter falling around her like soft rain. The light grew brighter and brighter.

Suddenly, there was a puff of pink smoke.

As Jaci looked on in amazement, the smoke cleared to reveal the most beautiful thing she had ever seen: a floating heart, red and gleaming, with big, kind eyes and a warm, friendly smile.

"Hello, Jaci My Dear!"
The heart could talk!

"My Dear, My Dear. Jaci, My Dear. There is nothing to fear. My name is Fairy Good Heart, and your tears brought me here."

The Fairy Good Heart spoke in a sing-song voice, so gentle and soothing. She wore a shimmering silver crown and carried a sparkly silver wand.

"I have come to tell you that a parent's love is something special— something that lasts, **forever and ever.**"

Jaci's lip began to tremble. She could feel the tears welling up inside her again. **"But Fairy Good Heart, how do you know?"**

The fairy beamed down at Jaci, and inside Jaci felt a warm, soft feeling, as if her whole body was **glowing.**

"Darling Jaci, a parent's love is like a magic spell.
It is the strongest, most powerful love in the world.
No matter what happens, your Mom will always be your Mom, and your Dad will always be your Dad. Nothing can change that.
Not anger nor sadness nor distance nor time."

As Jaci wiped her teary eyes, the Fairy Good Heart continued.

"Your parents are angry at one another, and you are afraid. It is normal to feel frightened. But always remember: they are not angry at you—and **they will always love you, forever and ever.**"

Jaci nodded. With the Fairy Good Heart by her side, she felt very safe.

"Fairy Good Heart, I will try to remember. But what if I forget? If you go away, I'm afraid I'll feel sad again."

"Oh Jaci, My Dear. I will always be with you."

Jaci rubbed her eyes. She could still hear Fairy Good Heart and see the pink glowing light—but where was she? Suddenly, the room was empty. There was no longer a floating heart above Jaci's bed. But instead, sitting by her side, there was a small, fuzzy heart, soft and plush, with a shimmering silver crown and a sparkly silver wand.

Then Jaci heard the voice again,
sweet and musical and filling up the whole room:

"I will stay by your side
every day and every night.
And when you feel sad or alone,
hold me tight and repeat these words..."

"My parents will love me
forever and ever, and
ever and ever."

Parent Prompts

Hello, My Dear:

You've just heard the story of Jaci's longest, most difficult night. Her parents are fighting, and she is confused and sad—but most of all, she is afraid her parents will stop loving her. When parents argue, it is common for children to feel this same fear. I want you and your parents to talk about Jaci's story, and answer the questions below. Talking can be difficult, but it is very important. The more we talk about our feelings, the sooner we will feel better and understand how much our parents love us, forever and ever.

1. Do you ever hear your parents fighting? When you do, what are you afraid of?
2. Why did Jaci think her parents would stop loving her? Do you ever feel this way about your parents?
3. Can you name two ways you know your parents will always love you?

Now remember, My Dear: your parents will love you forever and ever, and ever and ever. Can you say that out loud with me? "My parents will love me forever and ever, and ever and ever." Now say it one more time, as loud as you can!

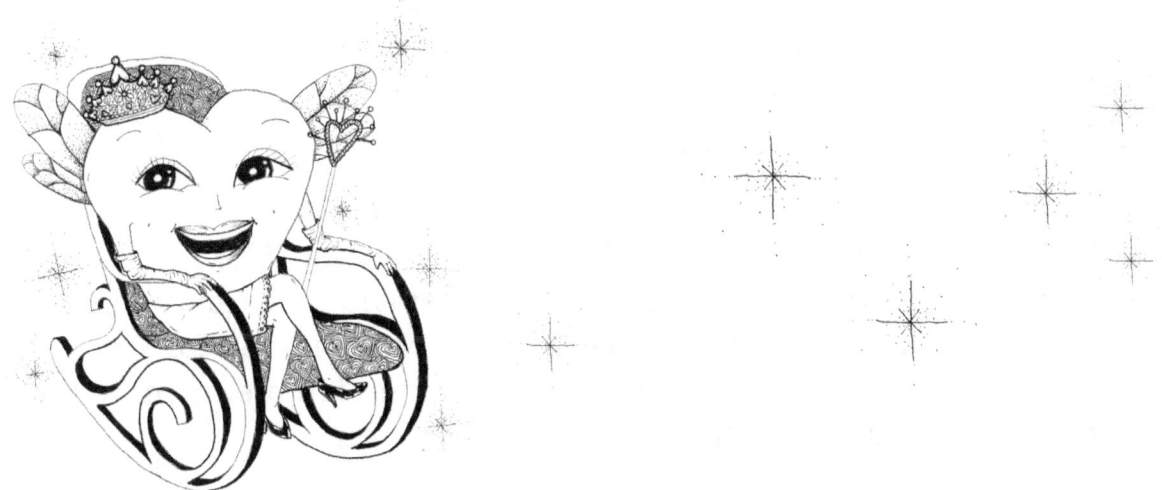

CHAPTER 2

The Bad News

The next day at school, Jaci couldn't wait for the bell to ring. She watched the clock on her classroom wall and wiggled in her seat with excitement. That morning, her Mom had told her that they would all be going out for ice cream after school—just Jaci, her Mom and her Dad. Jaci loved ice cream more than anything in the world. Anything, that is, except her parents.

On the way to the ice cream parlor,
Jaci thought about what she would order:
gumdrop ice cream,
chocolate waffle cone,
rainbow sprinkles, and
a cherry on top.

Gumdrop
was her favorite flavor,
and she hadn't had it in ages—
not since her last birthday,
when her Mom and Dad
had taken her out for a sundae.

When they arrived, Jaci ordered her cone: **"Gumdrop on a chocolate waffle cone with rainbow sprinkles, please!"** And her Mom smiled as the cashier handed Jaci her favorite treat, a mountain of pink and green and blue and purple with a bright red cherry on top. They sat down at a booth by the window, and Jaci took a big lick.

She beamed at her Mom with a mustache of sprinkles— but then frowned.

Something didn't seem right. Jaci's Mom kept looking out the window and biting her lip like she did when she was worried.

What could possibly be wrong?
How could she be worried at the ice cream parlor?

In an attempt to make her Mom smile, Jaci pulled Fairy Good Heart out of her backpack.

"Hey Mom, can my friend have some ice cream, too?"

Jaci danced the little plush heart across the table.

"Mmmm, she likes it as much as I do!"

It worked! Jaci's Mom smiled—though she also looked a bit confused.

"What a pretty toy you have there, Jaci! But… where did it come from?"

Before Jaci could answer, there was a tinkle of bells from the doorway.

"Daddy!" Jaci cried, jumping up to greet her Father.

"Aren't you going to get ice cream, Daddy?" Jaci asked. She knew her Father loved chocolate and bananas. But today, he shook his head no.

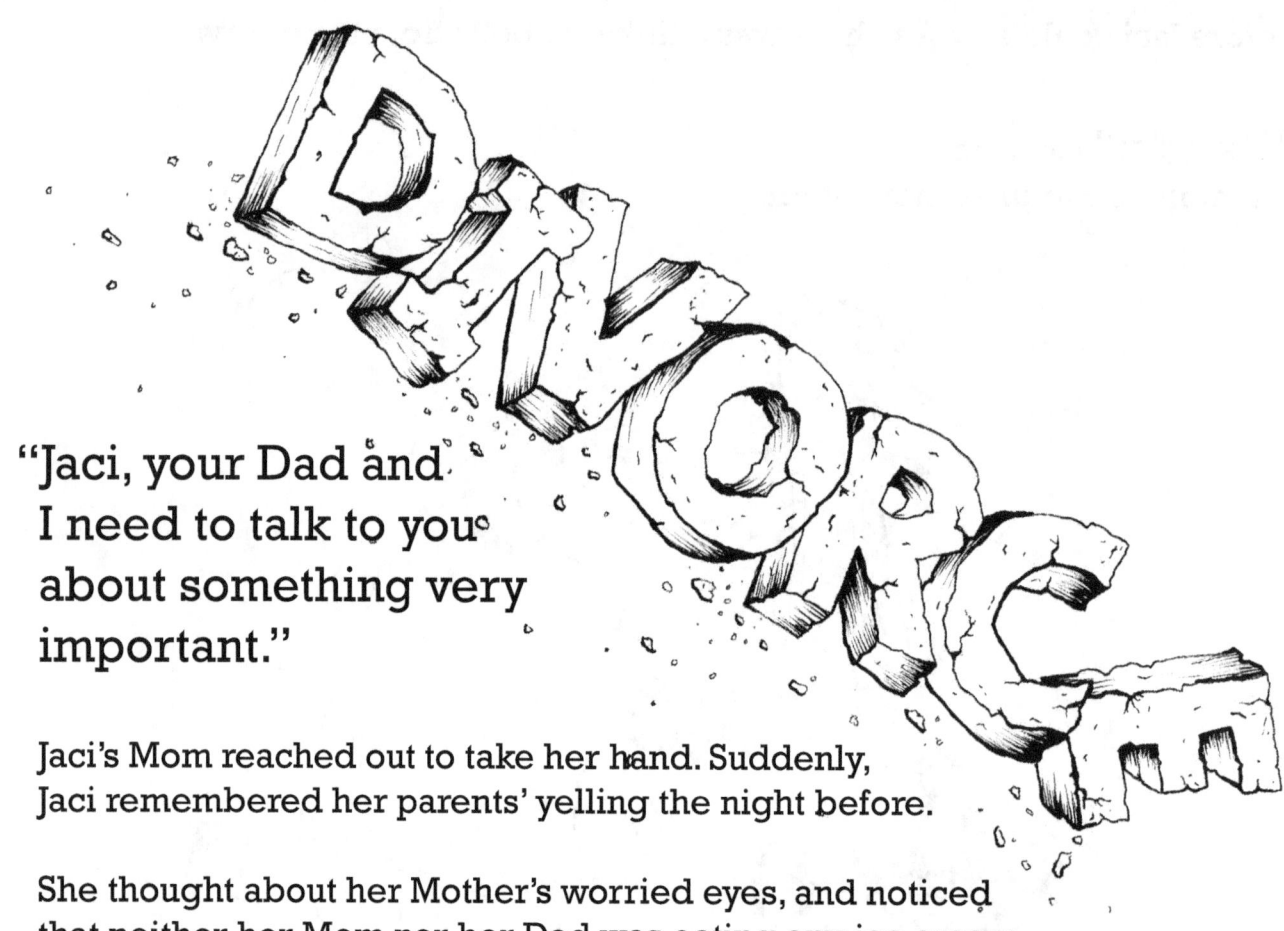

"Jaci, your Dad and I need to talk to you about something very important."

Jaci's Mom reached out to take her hand. Suddenly, Jaci remembered her parents' yelling the night before.

She thought about her Mother's worried eyes, and noticed that neither her Mom nor her Dad was eating any ice cream.

That word she'd heard upstairs in her room—"divorce"—echoed in her mind. Frightened, she drew her hand back and clutched the Fairy Good Heart tight against her chest.

"What we are going to tell you is very hard for us," her Mom said.

Your Dad and I have decided not to live together anymore. This is what grownups call "getting a divorce."

"Jaci, Honey, we want you to know that this decision has nothing to do with you.

Divorce is not your fault— and no matter what happens between your Father and I, **we both love you very, very much."**

Jaci felt stunned. She pushed away her ice cream and tried to fight the tears welling up behind her eyes. Her stomach hurt and her cheeks flushed. She felt many things—fear, sadness, and confusion—but certainly not love.

"If you stop living together, who is going to take care of me?" Jaci asked.

Her Dad pulled Jaci onto his lap and patted her back.

"We'll both take care of you, Sweetheart. That won't change. We'll just live in different homes, and we won't be married to each other anymore. That's all a divorce is."

Jaci's Mom reached towards her again, but Jaci jumped back, this time standing up and stepping away from both her parents.

"Why don't you love Dad?" she cried. The tears were coming faster now, and Jaci felt overwhelmed with sadness.

Just as her tears turned to sobs, Jaci heard a faint music in her ears:

"Remember, Jaci My Dear: your parents will love you forever and ever, and ever and ever."

She looked up and couldn't believe her eyes: right there above the table was the Fairy Good Heart, shining and smiling on a beautiful pink cloud.

In her astonishment, Jaci stopped crying. She waited for her parents to say something, but they both simply stood and wrapped their arms around her, blocking the Fairy Good Heart from view.

"Am I the only one who can see you?" Jaci whispered.

"My Dear, my Dear, Jaci My Dear," sang the voice, softer now, fading into the distance. Peeking out from her parents' embrace, Jaci saw that the fairy was gone. But her song lingered on just a little bit longer:

"Your parents love you a bunch. They love you a bunch. They love you so much. They love you a bunch!"

Parent Prompt

Hello, My Dear:

As you have just finished reading, Jaci's parents are getting a divorce. She has learned that divorce is when a mom and dad stop loving one another and decide to live in different homes. When Jaci learned about her parents' divorce, she had two main reactions: first, she was very sad and afraid that her parents would stop loving her; and second, she was angry with her Mother for breaking the bad news. Both of these reactions are completely normal for children whose parents are going through a divorce. So if you ever feel sad, afraid, confused or angry, just remember: these feelings are okay, and you don't need to hide them. Divorce is difficult for children and parents alike, and everyone will feel upset. The best way to feel better is to talk with your parents, and to ask questions to help you understand divorce more clearly.

1. Where were you when your parents told you that they were going to get a divorce? How did you feel?
2. Do you understand what "divorce" means? Do you have questions about it?
3. Do you feel anger toward either of your parents about getting a divorce?
4. What did you do after your parents told you they were getting a divorce? Did you talk to a sibling or friend, write in your diary, or meet with a counselor?

Now, My Dear: you are doing a great job sharing your feelings and talking about divorce with your parents. Remember that the more you talk, the better you will feel. Your parents will love you forever and ever, and ever and ever—no matter what you say or ask about divorce, even if it makes you feel confused or afraid! And talking will make your parents feel better, too. So keep up the good work!

Chapter 3

Moving Day

Several weeks passed. One by one the trees lost their leaves, and the weather grew cold. Jaci's Dad moved into an apartment across town, and Jaci's Mom put the family house up for sale.

The day finally came when Jaci and her Mom were set to move into their new apartment. A big storm had howled through the night before, burying the yard in a thick blanket of snow. As Jaci's Mom finished taping up boxes, Jaci sat huddled in the window seat under a blanket, a sketchbook on her lap and the Fairy Good Heart held tight against her chest.

With a tired sigh, Jaci's Mom came to sit beside her on the window seat.

"Hey Sweetie, what do you say to an ice cream break before we finish up all this packing?"

Jaci shook her head. "I don't like ice cream anymore," she said sadly. **"I never want to eat ice cream ever again."**

Just the thought of sprinkles and gumdrops made Jaci want to cry, reminding her of that horrible day when her parents first told her about the divorce.

She looked around the room at all the boxes—half filled with her Mother's things, the other half filled with stuff her Dad still needed to take to his apartment—and felt a big lump in her throat. Then she spotted her Dad's baseball mitt peeking out of the boxes.

It gave her an idea.

The phone rang, and Jaci's Mom went to answer it. As soon as she was gone, Jaci jumped out from under her blanket and grabbed the mitt. She shoved it into one of her Mom's boxes marked "Towels," then grabbed a piece of tape to shut the box up tight.

Maybe when he found it missing, her Dad would come over to get his mitt back…and if he and her Mom saw one another, they'd realize how much they missed being a family.

Just then, Jaci's Mom hung up the phone. Jaci hurried back to her spot on the window seat and snatched up her sketchbook again. When her Mom came back into the living room, Jaci was hard at work. She was proud of her secret plan—but still sad and angry with her Mom for making them move out of the house.

"What are you drawing, Jaci?" her Mother asked, returning to the window seat. Jaci frowned. Usually, she liked to draw horses and kittens and flowers and clouds. But lately, she had felt too sad for these things. Instead, she drew a picture of her Father and herself in their new house with sad and lonely expressions.

Taking the pad of paper from Jaci's lap, her Mother flipped through the pages. "Oh, Honey—are these pictures of you and your Father?"

Jaci nodded, hugging her Fairy Good Heart tight.

"Jaci, My Dearest Darling. I know you are sad. Your Father and I are sad, too."

Jaci's Mom wrapped her arms around Jaci and held her tight, so tight Jaci could smell her Mom's shampoo, like flowers and cinnamon.

"But remember:
This divorce is not your fault. You are a wonderful girl.
I love you more
than you will ever know—

and so does your Dad,
forever and ever,
and ever and ever."

Jaci hugged her Mother back. Ever since the ice cream parlor, she had felt so confused. She couldn't help but wonder if there was something she could have done to keep her parents from getting divorced: like being better in school, for instance, or faster at soccer practice, or quicker to clean up her room when her Mother asked her to.

But something about her Mother's voice, and her warm hug, and her sweet smelling hair, and the way she said those words just like Fairy Good Heart—

that she would love Jaci *"forever and ever, and ever and ever"*— made her feel better.

"**I love you too, Mom,**" Jaci said. She was still very sad, and she still hoped that her Dad would come over to pick up his baseball mitt. But between her Mom and Dad and the little Fairy Good Heart by her side, she was suddenly less afraid.

And that was a good feeling.

"I'll love you and Daddy forever and ever, and ever and ever."

Parent Prompt

Hello, My Dear:

As you can see, Jaci's life is changing. Her Dad moved out of the house, and now she and her Mom are moving, too. Jaci has gone through a lot of changes. And she is still sad—but little by little, she is becoming less confused and less angry at her parents about the divorce. She is also learning how to listen and talk with her parents about her feelings. This is the most important step of all—and one that you and your parents can take, too, using the questions below.

1. Did you have to move when your parents got divorced? What was one thing you liked about it? One thing you didn't like?
2. If you like to draw, do you draw pictures of your family? What do they look like? Do you share them with your parents?
3. Why do you think Jaci didn't want to eat ice cream anymore?
4. When you feel sad about your parents' divorce, what do you like to do to make yourself feel better?

Don't forget! In this chapter, Jaci learned something very special: that her parents will never stop loving her, no matter what happens. Remember that this is true for you and your parents as well. Now, read on to find out how the story ends. I'll give you a hint: Jaci learns how to be happy again!

CHAPTER 4
Two Houses for Jaci

A long winter turned into spring; and slowly, Jaci began to get used to her new life. While she missed her old house, she soon came to enjoy the excitement of having two completely different rooms—one at her Mom's apartment and one at her Dad's. She also noticed that both her parents seemed happier: her Mother less worried, her Father less tense. Jaci realized that maybe things really were better this way. She even snuck her Dad's hidden baseball mitt into her backpack and returned it to his new apartment during one of her weekend visits. After all, he might need it when they went to play at the park!

While she tried to keep it a secret at first, Jaci eventually told her friends about the divorce. She was nervous. What if they didn't like her anymore? But then she remembered that Amanda-Mia had two houses, too.

"Don't worry, Jaci,"

Amanda-Mia said.
The girls were playing on the swing set at recess,
trying to see who could swing the highest.

"I know how you feel.
I didn't want my parents to get divorced, either.
But sometimes, two houses can be fun!"

Jaci smiled. **"You're right, Amanda-Mia. My Dad's apartment even has a pool!"**

It was true: Jaci's Dad's apartment building had a pool and a tennis court—and best of all, Brandon's family lived in the same complex!

Every time she stayed with her Dad, Jaci got to play with Brandon and his dog, Arby, on the front lawn.

And when she went back to her Mom's apartment, she helped tend the patio garden full of tomatoes and bell peppers with Jessica, who lived just down the block.

Jaci loved living so close to her best friends, and felt relieved knowing that she wasn't the only girl whose parents were divorced.

But more than anything, she felt lucky: she had two parents who loved her, and that was better than any house or pool or tomato patch in the world.

At last, summer came. Jaci couldn't have been happier. School was out, the vacation days stretched ahead, long and sunny, and every day she got to play with her friends—at the pool, the tennis courts, the garden, or even trips to the zoo with her Mom and bike rides on the beach with her Dad.

It was Friday afternoon, and Jaci was waiting at the kitchen table for her Dad to come pick her up for the weekend. She saw his car pull up outside and shouted, **"Dad's here! Dad's here!"** as she scrambled out of her seat towards the door.

Her Mom followed her onto the front steps. **"Jaci! You forgot your little Fairy Good Heart."**

"Oh, yeah." Jaci spun around and ran back down the hall to her bedroom. There on her bed sat the Fairy Good Heart, smiling back at her from a soft nest of pillows.

Jaci paused. For the first time in months, she realized that she wasn't sad anymore—not even a little bit. She knew that her Mom loved her. She knew that her Dad loved her. She knew that both her parents would love her forever and ever, and ever and ever.

Maybe she didn't need the Fairy Good Heart to keep her company this weekend, after all.

Jaci grabbed a stuffed rabbit off her dresser and plopped him on the bed next to Fairy Good Heart.

"This is your new friend, Mr. Bunny," she said.

"Mr. Bunny, meet Fairy Good Heart. I think the two of you will like each other very much and be best friends forever."

And with that,
Jaci turned and dashed out the door and down the hall towards her Mother, who stood waiting with Jaci's backpack and a wide grin on her face.

"Where's your toy?" she asked.

"She doesn't need to come with me, Mom. She said she'd rather stay home with you and Mr. Bunny this time."

Jaci skipped out the door, then turned back to give her Mother a big hug.

"Bye, Mom! I love you. And hey—could we maybe go out for ice cream when you pick me up on Sunday?"

"That sounds wonderful, Sweetie. I'd love to get ice cream."

Jaci's Mom waved goodbye. "I love you, too—*forever and ever, and ever and ever.*"

Parent Prompt

My Dear,

We've come to the end of the story—and at last, Jaci is happy again! She knows that her parents love her, and that her new life isn't bad or strange; it is simply different.

I hope you've enjoyed hearing about Jaci's experience, and the lessons she learned with help from the Fairy Good Heart. Please read the final questions below, and remember to ask your parents any questions that came up as you followed along with Jaci's story.

1. How did Jaci overcome her fear and sadness about divorce?
2. What made Jaci realize that she wasn't alone in having divorced parents?
3. Do you know other kids whose parents are divorced?
4. Do you talk to your friends about your own parents' divorce?
5. Jaci felt lucky because she learned that both her parents loved her, no matter what. What are some things your parents do to make you feel loved?

What's the moral of this story? It is that your parents will love you, no matter what happens. Even if they stop loving each other and get a divorce, they will never stop loving you. If you ever feel lonely or sad or frightened or confused, talk to your Mom and Dad and let them know how you are feeling. And most of all, remember: that your parents will love you forever and ever, and ever and ever!

APPENDIX

FAIRY GOOD HEART PAPER DOLL

Instructions: Cut out the Fairy Good Heart paper doll. Use tape to assemble the pieces. If you would like to have movable arms and legs, insert a small brass fastener. For video instructions, visit www.FairyGoodHeart.com/Kids.

www.FairyGoodHeart.com

FAIRY GOOD HEART™
Order Form

Products   Qty   Price   Subtotal

Paperback
Fables of Fairy Good Heart:
Divorce - A Parent's Love
Lasts Forever $12.95

E-Book (Download)
Fables of Fairy Good Heart:
Divorce - A Parent's Love
Lasts Forever $4.95

Stuffed FGH Toy
With built-in pouch
for parent kiss notes.
10" x 10" $12.95

Bundle Discount:
Paperback Book AND
Stuffed FGH Toy $22.95

Subtotal: _____

CA residents add 10% Tax: _____

(S & H) Add $4.95 for 1st item
$1.00 each additional: _____

TOTAL: _____

How to Order

Online: www.FairyGoodHeart.com

Phone: 1-858-805-1190

By mail: Send this form and check to:
          Fairy Good Heart LLC
          1315 Torrey Pines Rd
          La Jolla, CA 92047

Make checks payable to: Fairy Good Heart LLC

Name:_____

Shipping Address:_____

City:_____ State:____

Zip_____ Phone:_____

Email:_____

www.ingramcontent.com/pod-product-compliance
Lightning Source LLC
Chambersburg PA
CBHW082247300426
44110CB00039B/2468